02164

J
910
.9
Bla

Blackwood, Alan, 1932-
    The age of exploration / Alan Blackwood ; illustrated
by John James. -- Hove, [England] : Wayland, 1990.
    24 p. : col. ill., maps. -- (Beginning history)

Includes index.
Bibliography: p. 23.
03828646   ISBN:1852107820

1. Discoveries (in geography) - History. 2. Explorers. I.
James, John. II. Title

10753   90APR23   06/se   1-00509413

BEGINNING HISTORY

THE AGE OF EXPLORATION

Alan Blackwood

Illustrated by John James

BEGINNING HISTORY

The Age of Exploration
Crusaders
Egyptian Pyramids
Greek Cities
Medieval Markets
Norman Castles

Roman Cities
Roman Soldiers
Saxon Villages
Tudor Sailors
Victorian Children
Viking Explorers

All words that appear in **bold** are explained in the glossary on page 22.

Series Editor: Rosemary Ashley
Book Editor: Anna Girling
Designer: Helen White

First published in 1990 by Wayland (Publishers) Limited, 61 Western Road,
Hove, East Sussex BN3 1JD

British Library Cataloguing in Publication Data
Blackwood, Alan, *1932–*
The age of exploration.
1. Exploration, History
I. Title   II. Series
910′.9

ISBN 1 85210 782 0

Typeset by Kalligraphics Limited, Horley, Surrey.
Printed in Italy by G. Canale & C.S.p.A., Turin.
Bound in Belgium by Casterman, S.A.

CONTENTS

TRADE ROUTES OLD AND NEW

During the **Middle Ages**, **traders** from Europe went to Asia to bring back **spices**, jewels, furs and silks. They set up trade routes across Africa and overland to China.

But from the end of the eleventh century, the **Christians** in Europe and the **Muslims** from the East fought a series of wars called the **Crusades**. Muslim armies conquered much of the Middle East and North Africa, cutting off Europe from the trade routes to Asia in the East.

Camels, laden with spices and other goods, plod across the Arabian desert.

Because Europe was cut off from the East, Portugal, at the other end of Europe, grew in importance. It faced the Atlantic Ocean, away from the Muslim lands around the Mediterranean Sea. In the fourteenth century, Prince Henry of Portugal saw how important this was and encouraged sailors to find new trade routes. He became known as Henry the Navigator and the great age of exploration began with him.

HENRY THE NAVIGATOR

Prince Henry studied the design of sailing ships. In those days the ships were made of wood and had masts and sails. Henry designed better sails so that the ships were easier to

Above *Henry the Navigator. The Portuguese prince encouraged exploration, though he never set sail himself.*

Right *Lisbon, the Portuguese capital, was a busy port in the sixteenth century.*

handle and could move faster. He also drew maps and improved the **navigation** equipment which helped sailors find their way at sea.

The men who first set sail from Portugal into the unknown were very brave. There were frightening stories that the sea in the south turned into a sticky soup under the heat of the sun. There was a danger of scurvy, a terrible illness which sailors got from eating a poor diet. In bad weather the ships leaked and the crew got cold and wet.

Below *A busy Portuguese shipyard at the time of Henry the Navigator. New and better ships were needed for the voyages of exploration.*

AROUND THE CAPE

In 1487, the explorer Bartolomeo Diaz set off from Portugal to lead a new expedition down the west coast of Africa.

Diaz made his way down the coast, across the **equator** and into the southern **hemisphere**. Then, strong winds blew his two ships far away from land and south into the Roaring Forties. These are the stormy seas that lie south of the equator. The men were cold, hungry, ill and frightened. They believed they had reached the end of the world and would never see their homes again.

Bartolomeo Diaz's ship struggles through stormy seas around southern Africa.

At last, Diaz managed to steer his ships around the Cape of Good Hope, which is the southernmost tip of Africa. He wanted to go on, but his crew had had enough. Many men died of illness and starvation before the expedition got home in 1488.

ON TO INDIA

Below *Muslims attack da Gama's ships near Mombasa. They did not want him to steal their trade with India.*

About ten years later, in 1497, Vasco da Gama set sail from Portugal. Like Diaz, he was looking for a new sea-route around Africa and on to the East.

Vasco da Gama planned his expedition very carefully. He managed to navigate his ships round the Cape of Good Hope and up the east coast of Africa to the port of Mombasa, where he had to fight off attacks from Muslim traders. Then

he sailed across the Indian Ocean to the coast of India.

Vasco da Gama was welcomed as a hero when he got back to Portugal in 1499. He had faced storms, and long periods when his ships were **becalmed**. He had lost two ships and more than half his men had died from scurvy. But he had sailed to India – and back again!

Left *The beautiful west coast of India, which Vasco da Gama reached in 1498.*

WESTWARD TO THE INDIES

Sailors navigated by measuring the angle of the sun.

Below *This map is dated 1490.*

While Bartolomeo Diaz and Vasco da Gama were sailing around Africa, other explorers had even more daring plans. They were sure that the world was round, like a ball, so they thought it would be easier to reach China and the Indies by sailing due west, instead of all the way around

12

Africa. The 'Indies' was the name given in those days to India and the Spice Islands, which are now called the Moluccas.

These explorers drew up maps of the world that included most of Europe, large parts of Asia and some of the coast of Africa. The trouble was that they knew nothing about the **continent** we now know as America, and they believed the world was smaller than it really is.

Below Navigators study maps and plan to sail westwards around the world. They hoped to reach the Indies and China.

CHRISTOPHER COLUMBUS

Christopher Columbus believed he could reach the Indies by sailing west. In fact, he reached the continent we know as America – but he had no idea what he had found!

Columbus came from Italy, but his famous expeditions were paid for by the King and Queen of Spain. He set sail from Spain on his first voyage of exploration in 1492 with his **flagship** the *Santa Maria* and two smaller ships. They stopped first at the

Canary Islands, off the coast of Africa, then headed west across the Atlantic Ocean.

Two months later they reached the island of San Salvador in the Bahamas. From there they sailed on into the Caribbean Sea, where they landed on the islands of Cuba and Hispaniola.

Columbus arrived back in Spain in 1493. He brought with him strange plants and animals. He also brought people he had captured on the islands. He called these people Indians, because he thought he had reached the Indies.

Christopher Columbus lands on the island of San Salvador. He had reached the Americas, although he did not realize it.

THE AMERICAS

The Atlantic coast of South America, much of which was mapped by Vespucci.

Below *People feared that monsters lived in unknown lands.*

After Columbus's first voyage, other explorers decided to plan their own expeditions across the Atlantic Ocean. One of these explorers was an Italian called Amerigo Vespucci.

Vespucci left Spain in 1499 and sailed with four ships across the Atlantic, at last reaching South America near the mouth of the River Amazon. He then headed south,

making maps of the coastline as he went, before returning home.

In 1501 Vespucci led a second expedition. This time he sailed much further down the coast of South America, as far south as the country we now call Argentina. By then he believed Columbus was wrong in thinking these lands were part of the Indies. He was sure they belonged to a completely different continent. He named the continent America, after his own first name.

Below *Vespucci's ships sail near the mouth of the River Amazon.*

A NORTHWEST PASSAGE

A huge iceberg towers over John Cabot's ship off the coast of North America. One of the masts has broken in the stormy weather.

Other explorers thought they would find a new route to China and the Indies by sailing north of America. They called this route the Northwest Passage.

John Cabot, an Italian sailor who lived in England, tried to find a Northwest Passage. He and his son Sebastian made two voyages and sailed to the icy coasts we now know as Newfoundland and Nova Scotia. In 1498 John Cabot did not return from

an expedition. He was probably killed in a **shipwreck**.

The Portuguese explorer Gaspar Corte Real and his brother made maps of the coasts of Greenland and Labrador, but they too died in the bitter northern weather. The Frenchman Jacques Cartier explored the coast of Canada. In 1535 he sailed up the St Lawrence River as far as what is now the city of Montreal.

FIRST AROUND THE WORLD

Below *Map showing the routes of four of the explorers.*

In 1519 the Portuguese navigator Ferdinand Magellan set sail to try to find a way around America. He took a **fleet** of five ships.

He managed to sail around the tip of South America, through the channel which is now called the Straits of Magellan. Then, for nearly four months, his ships sailed on and on across the vast Pacific Ocean.

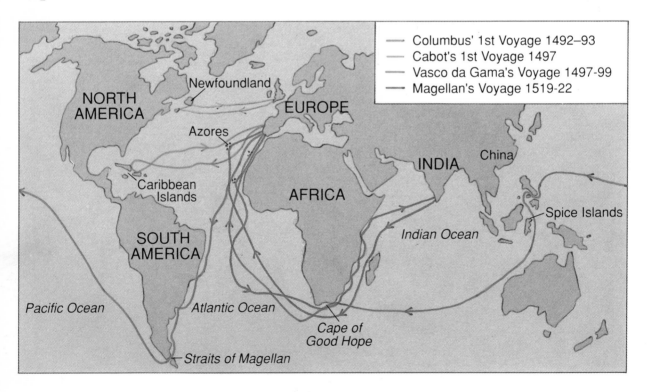

Legend:
- Columbus' 1st Voyage 1492–93
- Cabot's 1st Voyage 1497
- Vasco da Gama's Voyage 1497-99
- Magellan's Voyage 1519-22

Map labels: NORTH AMERICA, Newfoundland, EUROPE, Azores, Caribbean Islands, INDIA, China, AFRICA, Spice Islands, SOUTH AMERICA, Indian Ocean, Pacific Ocean, Atlantic Ocean, Cape of Good Hope, Straits of Magellan

Many of his men died of hunger and scurvy. They were so hungry they even ate rats.

At last they reached land, but Magellan was killed by local people in the Philippine Islands. In the end, only a few survivors sailed on in a single ship, the *Victoria*, around the Cape of Good Hope and back home. It had taken them three years to sail right around the whole world. Magellan's expedition had proved the world was round, and larger than anyone had thought.

Below *Many of Magellan's crew died of scurvy or starvation as they sailed across the vast Pacific Ocean.*

GLOSSARY

Becalmed When sailing ships cannot move because there is no wind to blow them along.

Christians People who believe in Jesus Christ.

Continent One of the seven very large areas of land in the world. They are Asia, Australasia, Africa, Europe, North and South America and Antarctica.

Crusades The series of wars fought during the Middle Ages between Christians and Muslims for possession of the Holy Land (the country we now call Israel and surrounding lands).

Equator The imaginary line round the centre of the Earth, which is equal distance from the North and South Poles.

Flagship The most important ship in a group of ships.

Fleet A group of ships that sail together.

Hemisphere Half a sphere or ball, particularly the two halves of the Earth, north and south of the equator.

Middle Ages The period in history from about AD 1000 to AD 1450.

Muslims Followers of the Islamic religion.

Navigation Finding your way at sea by looking at the sun, moon and stars.

Shipwreck The destruction of a ship by bad weather or a disaster at sea.

Spice A strong-tasting substance, such as pepper, used in cooking. Long ago, spices were used to preserve food or hide the taste of food that was going bad.

Trader Someone who buys goods and sells them again to earn money.

BOOKS TO READ

Columbus and the Age of Exploration by Stewart Ross (Wayland, 1985)
Exploration in History by Sheila Robertson (Wayland, 1984)
The Explorers by Richard Humble (Time-Life Books, 1978)
Ferdinand Magellan by Alan Blackwood (Wayland, 1985)
Man the Navigator by E.W. Anderson (Priory Press, 1973)

Picture acknowledgements

The illustrations in this book were supplied by: Bruce Coleman 11 (Gerald Cubitt), 16 (top) (L. C. Marigo); Michael Holford 6 (top); Ronald Sheridan 6 (bottom), 12 (top and bottom), 16 (bottom). The map on page 20 was supplied by Jenny Hughes.

INDEX